Holy Friend

JOY RASH

DENVER, COLORADO

Outskirts Press, Inc.
http://www.outskirtspress.com

ISBN: 978-1-4787-3500-7

Outskirts Press and the "OP" logo are trademarks belonging to Outskirts Press, Inc.

PRINTED IN THE UNITED STATES OF AMERICA

I dedicate this book to
my dear husband, Alan,
who happens to also be
my best friend on earth.

Those sweet souls who have always brought
the sparkle of sunshine and the blessing of happiness
to my world,
my wonderful family –
three sons, their wives,
thirteen grandchildren, and
two great-granddaughters-
have daily painted for me a living mural,
perfectly depicting the central thought of
"My Holy Friend":
God's endless gifts
to us all.

Holy Spirit

My heartfelt thanks to my sponsors,
Thomas Markley and Martha Ahlmann,
for their faith in the concept
and for much needed coaching;

and to special friends,
Nancy Smythe and Sylvia Hansen,
for their undying encouragement in my life,
as well as in the writing of this book.

I am also especially grateful to
Judy Dadabo
for her kind and tireless artistic consultation
and to Les Cunliffe © 2011
for the use of his art on the cover.

Interior art work is presented
with the gracious consent of Inmagine.com.

A special "Thank you" to
Brie Curtis,
of Outskirts Press,
whose blend of kindness and expertise
significantly contributed
to the publication of this book.

A CARING COMPANION
FOR THE LONG WALK HOME –

that was what I always wanted, a special friend to hold my hand during the celebrations and challenges that would be part of my life experience.

I never thought of God in that role. My picture of him was as a judge, keeping a record of all my mistakes.

But then one day, in a blessed encounter that could have been brought about by no other than God, I realized that my belief was out of sync with the Good News Jesus came to proclaim. Consequently, I took another look at what Christ actually taught, and began to see his message in a new way.

<u>Jesus declared that God is my loving and merciful Father.</u> This truth alone started to untangle for me the kinks and knots in the yarn from which is woven the tapestry showing his plan for our salvation.

That was when the dawn broke, revealing the fact that, because of my chronic sinfulness, God had to justify his unconditional acceptance and deep love for me. His divine wisdom designed a method through his Son's sacrificial gift. This is the way he sees past all the wrong things I've ever said and done, or am yet to say and do, even those whose only existence is in my thought world, straight through to the perfection he implanted in me when I was created. Wonder of wonders, at long last, it all made perfect sense!

The most dramatic revelation came next. It suddenly became obvious that the resurrection of Jesus Christ, in addition to being the irrefutable proof of his victory over death, really meant more than that. I finally knew in the core of my being that if Jesus of Nazareth had been re-born into **ETERNAL LIFE** two thousand years ago, **he is still alive today;** in fact, I believe he stays quite busy fulfilling his original intent: protecting, inspiring, encouraging, and interceding for me and all believers every day.

As a result of this fresh awareness, my life began to change. I prayed differently, dropping formal terms, like "thee", "thou", and "thy". I quickly found great comfort in talking to our Lord exactly the way I speak to a really close friend. Before long I was also praying more frequently, totally forgetting my earlier fear that God is too busy for my small problems.

I also noticed that in Scripture there are no subjects that are off-limits for prayer. King David and others who wrote the Old Testament book of Psalms showed this by sharing with the Almighty every raw emotion the events in their regular lives provoked. Following their example, I started to tell the King of

Kings everything. I prayed when I was sad, happy, angry, afraid, and especially when I felt I had been treated unfairly.

<u>And God listened!</u> I know this because it was meaningfully demonstrated. Instead of my constant concern for the problems that used to cause so much trouble, their solutions soon emerged as the focus of my attention.

(CONFESSION: These life changes were undoubtedly also due to the transformation God was bringing about deep in my heart.)

In this book, I am pleased to share with you the happiness I have found by growing closer to my "special friend" – the very one for whom I had always searched. Actually, I call him **MY HOLY FRIEND.** He has become indispensable to me. I would not like to think of life without our regular chats. On the following pages I share my part of some of them.

But may I first give you some information which I hope will ease your reading?

1. Biblical quotations in "My Holy Friend" are from the New International Version, a less formal Bible translation, which aims at urging a closer relationship between the reader and our Father. One way its editors achieve this more comfortable style is by reversing the earlier, more traditional practice of capitalizing

all pronouns used to refer to God, as well as words descriptive of him. I have followed their lead in my psalms, in the hope that it conveys this heightened sense of intimacy, still wrapped in utter reverence, which I feel for the Lord of the Universe.

2. In addition, I have used a variety of titles for God in these modern day psalms. The significance of names in general was recently explained by Dr. David Jeremiah, prominent radio and television evangelist and pastor of a large church in San Diego, California. "Names can be a doorway into knowing who a person is, and that is certainly true of God." Especially in Biblical times, they were often chosen to suggest the nature of the person named. So besides achieving an increased and less ritualistic connection to our heavenly Father, I also invite my reader to grow in familiarity with the Christian concept of the Trinity, and the many names growing out of it.

For many years, this basic tenet of our faith was difficult for me to get a handle on. A recent explanation presented by Dr. Alister McGrath, Theology Professor at Oxford University in England, helped me see its meaning more clearly. Dr. McGrath emphasizes that, while it is important to avoid projecting this doctrine into a fallacious belief in a trio of deities, it nevertheless enhances our understanding to think of a single God who fills man's three greatest needs: creation, accomplished by God the Father; salvation, provided through the sacrifice of Jesus Christ the Son; and the perpetual presence of the Deity, as promised by Jesus in John 14:16 and fulfilled by the Holy Spirit.

One God, filling three distinct roles, each one always accessible to us, and answering to a variety of titles.

Growth in my grasp of this concept has greatly increased my feeling of connection to all that is the one true God.

Now as you turn these pages, please accept the call found in James 4:8 --

"Come near to God and he will come near to you."

PSALM 1

I have seen your personal involvement
In the lives of your children, Lord.
You have lent divine assistance
By refining and nurturing gifts
With which you originally blessed them.

These talents and abilities
Cover a wide variety of interests.
Some are barely noted by the holder,
Some ardently cherished,
With total focus and hope invested
Toward the fulfillment
Of a special dream.

You provided each of these blessings
As a dear act of love,
Much as any devoted father might do.

How they are used,
Whose glory they applaud,
Generously left for the recipient
To determine, Jehovah,
Is but one more facet
Of your grace.
Judgment on how an endowment

1

Is employed is mostly left unspoken;
I have no desire to alter that.

However, Son of God,
Since we have become fast friends,
My heart's desire
Remains to bring you glory.
It seems beautifully fitting then
That I should choose
To re-direct toward you,
The divine provider,
The natural result flowing
From the bounty of your generosity.

Nothing would please me more
Than to create an act of worship
From the abilities with which
You have honored me.

If, before I depart from the beauty
You created on this earth,
I could paint with words
A portrait of your magnificence,
Including the sweet and tender ways
You work within each life,
I would be tremendously gratified,
Presenting that work as a tribute.

You have many times
Granted me opportunities
To use the abilities, Abba,
With which you endowed me.

On the following pages,
I attempt once again
To assist my brothers and sisters
In recognizing the infinite,
Sublimely lovely dividends available
For vastly enhancing their lives,
Once they accept your incomparable
Plan for them in eternity.

Because I have welcomed you
Into my life, Holy Father,
Embracing with everlasting gratitude
The sacrifice of your son Jesus,
You have awakened my consciousness
To the scope of your action in my life.

Ruler of my heart,
I lift my highest praise to you;
I offer you unlimited gratitude,
King of Glory.

Thank you for the gift.
Thank you for allowing me
To unwrap it.

 In all my prayers for all of you, I always pray with joy because of your partnership in the gospel from the first day until now, being confident of this, that he who began a good work in you will carry it on to completion until the day of Christ Jesus. Philippians 1:4-6

PSALM 2

Holy Spirit

Daytime in the past
Was often followed, Prince of Peace,
By seemingly endless nights,
Slumber a reluctant ally.

Until I found your friendship,
My mind often roamed the universe
In my nocturnal misery,
Confronting challenges
Yet to show themselves
When the sun shines brightly,
Besides those presently demanding
My undivided daytime attention.

Joyfully, stirring and stewing
Are no longer necessary, Comforter,
Because I know you.
Our close connection
Has taught me the value
Of each moment.

When sleep plays the fugitive,
As sometimes happens in our society
Of abundant technological stimulation,
I now see the occasion

As you intend it:
Serendipitous moments
To welcome your inspiration.

The hours when true rest is elusive
Are perfect for communing with you;
Your unending presence
For counsel or comfort
Cancels the need for a callback.

Master, you make your love obvious
By your constant accessibility.

I exalt you;
I honor you.
I extol your mercy and grace
From the top of the highest hill.

 For through him we both have access to the
Father by one Spirit. Ephesians 2:18

PSALM 3

Jesus, I am elated that,
Besides your home in paradise,
Thankfully, you also reside
Actively,
Joyously,
In my heart!

From that command post,
You are the filter
Through which I experience life.

You perfectly meet countless needs:
Encourager,
Teacher,
Healer,
Shepherd,
Legal advisor,
Disciplinarian,
Mentor,
Judge,
Life coach,
Financial consultant,
Prophet,
Marriage counselor,
Civics professor,

Advocate,
Child psychologist,
Muse,
Grief therapist,
Social director,
Time-management instructor,
Confidant,
And, above all,
Best Friend.

Even though you are
Actively involved in my life,
The inevitable pain of earthly living
Has not vanished.

In fact, my devotion to you
Has dictated rejection by both of us
Of some roles which might appear logical
By man's standards.
You consistently refuse to be
A trailblazer for me, Counselor,
Eliminating much danger
From those battle zones
Where my soul's sanctification
Is dependent on enduring
The sharp trial of struggle.

Despite any imagined
Position of entitlement
Stemming from devotion to you,
You have declared unacceptable

Any potential attitude
Of superiority
Over worldly siblings.

Even when my spirit
Is legitimately weighed down
By mistreatment, Everlasting Father,
You firmly forbid my assumption
Of the additional baggage
Of presumed victimization.

With the bittersweet gift of free will,
You allow me the luxury
Of choice in attitude and deed;
Still, you disallow my escape
From the consequences of those decisions.

I gratefully welcome the innumerable ways
You brighten my experiences
By your vibrant presence each day.
Thank you, Spirit of Life,
For continuing to guide me.

"But when he, the Spirit of truth comes, he will guide you into all truth. He will not speak on his own; he will speak only what he hears, and he will tell you what is yet to come." John 16:13

PSALM 4

Holy Spirit

You are abundantly more
Than a holy chess master, Yahweh.
Yet you constantly move souls
Like pawns and kings,
Precisely producing the best outcome
For each player
On your universal board.

It is little wonder
That the God of all that is
Executes this task with perfection.
The person being moved,
As well as the watchful bystander
Observing the fulfillment of your plan,
Is forever amazed by the thrill
Of the accomplishment of your goal
For each of us.

Only an omnipotent,
Omniscient,
Omnipresent,
Thoroughly loving ruler

Could consistently
Evoke the best result
For each of us.

And we know that in all things God works for the
good of those who love him, who have been called
to his purpose. Romans 8:28

PSALM 5

Oh, God of unending faithfulness,
My loyal friend and protector,
You tuck me in at night
Beneath the millions of milky ways
You have created.
Through the darkness you stand guard;
No harm can touch me.
As morning spreads its first bright rays,
You prepare me for the day,
Dressing me in energy and enthusiasm.

Without restriction or disclaimer,
Your love flows freely, Lamb of God.
Your heart constantly reaches for mine
In a communion only dreamed of by mortals.

When I live at my best,
Or even when my dark side
Overwhelms my higher instincts,
Your gentle arms sustain me.

Your eye is unimpeded.
In a single moment
It plumbs from the depths of the sea
To the brilliance of the farthest star.

You view my life story,
Always tempering judgment with tender grace.

Spirit of Truth, as a source of guidance,
You are more reliable than the finest compass.
Whether I bask in the sunshine of success,
Or struggle in failure's deep, dark pit,
I find you by my side.
Celebration without you rings hollow.
In distress, only your comfort heals.

One may ask why I am so confident, Lord,
Of the many dimensions of your character.

The image imparted by your son Jesus
Beautifully illustrates your nature.
Knowing him provides a picture of you.

 "The Lord your God is with you, he is mighty to save. He will take great delight in you, he will quiet you with his love, he will rejoice over you with singing." Zephaniah 3:17

PSALM 6

Holy Spirit

What an awakening for me, mighty God,
Was the truth that your Son,
Jesus Christ, is alive!
The revelation continues to resonate
Throughout my universe!

His resurrection had already established
Concrete proof of my eternal life.
It had long been obvious
That you seated him in heaven
So that I might recognize it
As my home.

The passion of that promise
Has swelled into a blazing flame,
Inspiring my heart,
Directing my steps.

How incredibly brave,
How incomparably selfless
Was he, my Savior,
To endure the agony
In order to help me see
That I, too, will overcome death!

In spite of this priceless gift,
The enemy crouches
Just outside the entrance
To your haven of eternal bliss,
Clamoring for attention.
He taunts me with the reminder:
I must pass through his
Snare of suffering
Before I arrive at home.

Without your merciful grace, Jehovah,
Peace and happiness would remain
Just beyond my outstretched arms.
Because of your Son's sacrifice,
The chasm between you and me
Has been reduced
To a mere skip and a hop.
The ugly, scowling countenance
Of the fallen sentry
Is eclipsed by your brilliant radiance
Transcending the divide.

Though daily challenges
Often stagger me, Holy One,
The live Christ is now
The axis on which my life turns.
His constant nearness,
Coupled with the transforming thought
That he resides wholly free
Of any finite concept of time,
Fuels my slow but certain progress

In growing toward the goal you set for me:
Becoming more like Jesus.

It is heartening that he remains today
As vibrant as when the cattle heard
The babe's cry in the straw of the manger;
As authoritative as when the scribes recognized
The truth of the boy's reasoning in the synagogue;
As powerful as when the lame and the blind received
The Rabbi's healing;
As profound as when the masses absorbed
The Master's teaching;
As delightful as when the disciples relished
The friend's companionship;
As undefeated as when the governor witnessed
The prisoner's peace;
As loving as when the thief received
The Lord's forgiveness.

Dear Father, your Son, Jesus,
Lives and breathes
Within my soul!

Christ is alive!
Praise our infinite Father God!

 Therefore he is able to save completely those who come to God through him, because he always lives to intercede for them. Hebrews 7:25

PSALM 7

You continually bless me, Father,
Designing for me
A far richer life than I deserve.
The people you have placed
Beside me on this path
Nurture my spirit and sweeten my days.

In addition to many material favors,
Your most splendid gift, Abba,
Is wanting to be my friend.
By mortal reasoning,
Such intimacy is inconsistent,
Given the inescapable paradox:
The proof of love we each render
Is disproportionate.

My weak mortality,
With its bare means of expression,
Awkwardly hems in my ability
To offer the unrestrained adoration
Surging within my heart.

But through your divine flexibility,
You monitor the earth's steady rotation,
Simultaneously applying supernatural vision

To enjoyment of the vibrant hues you painted
On the wings of the butterfly.

No power is mightier than yours,
Yet no touch gentler.
Your knowledge surpasses
The sum of the contents
Of all of man's hard drives.
Still, by employing utmost finesse,
You seek and find
The secret place in my heart,
Healing the hurt I have buried there.

How extraordinary a God you are,
Lord of Lords!
How dear a friend!

 "I no longer call you servants, because a servant does not know his master's business. Instead I have called you friends, for everything that I learned from my Father I have made known to you." John 15:15

PSALM 8

El Shaddai, wishing to praise you
Is as natural as the desire to breathe.
The rush of blessings
You have poured into my life
Propels my spirit toward
Spending all my days honoring you.

Besides numerous tangible gifts,
I am grateful for your incredible patience,
In the face of my stubborn pride.
Instead of giving up on me,
You gently correct my errors,
Refining my spirit
Through ingenious teaching.

The inability I display
To see people and events
From your perspective, Redeemer,
Always expecting them to fit
A profile I have constructed for them,
Must cause you great pain.
Still you repeatedly forgive me.

Spirit of Grace, even in my darkest hours,
When you have convicted me of sin,

You offer hope:
Hope that yesterday's mistakes
Have been pardoned and erased;
Hope that I still have a specific purpose;
Hope that when I reach for your hand,
I will find you.

You have showered me with subtle mercies,
Sometimes hidden
By apparent frustrations.

With the passing of time,
The sharpness of my eyesight
Has become diminished,
Causing increased dependence on others.
This has unexpectedly
Deepened relationships.

Paradoxically, with a limited
Field of physical vision,
My insight in matters of the heart
Has been enhanced.

Sounds seem more distant now.
When I am surrounded by others,
Spoken thoughts are often drowned out
By the encircling clutter of chatter.
But you, Wonderful Counselor,
Routinely cut through the cacophony
To whisper truths I need to hear.

Yahweh, my sincere wish to praise you
Is unfortunately inhibited
By a meager capacity for expression.

Lauding you through song is ineffective,
Since the croaking noise
Spilling out of my throat
Would shame a respectable frog.
My fingers move so laboriously
On keyboard or strings
That a chorus of lively hallelujahs
Would be transformed into a plodding dirge.

Perhaps my body once moved gracefully.
However, any attempt to employ it today
In celebration of your beauty
Would be interpreted as farce,
Not worship.

Maybe my best way to honor you, Holy Friend,
Is by reminding my brothers and sisters
That you are the remedy
For all mortal angst.

This is my adoring praise to you,
Father of my heart.

Through Jesus, therefore, let us continually offer
to God a sacrifice of praise - the fruit of lips that
confess his name. Hebrews 13:15

20

PSALM 9

Resting securely in your unearned,
Extravagant love, Lord,
I have gotten a glimpse
Of the pure happiness
Which is a central part
Of your plan for me.

Beautiful beyond comparison,
It comes tenderly wrapped
In the invitation
To receive even greater benefits
By completely surrendering
My life to you.

However, you have set before me
An unlikely task.
Even my national heritage has preached
Self-sufficiency
As the hallmark of success.

My individual personality
Seems only content, Holy Spirit,
When exercising sole authority
Over the events of my days.

Jesus, relinquishing control
Of this temporal adventure
Feels unnatural --
Too much to ask.

Yet I can clearly see
By reviewing my life story,
Each of my most bitter struggles
Was stained by disappointment,
Even when success seemed near.

In contrast, Good Shepherd,
Your power, when I have allowed it
To direct my days,
Has rewarded me generously
With accomplishment,
Whether material or spiritual,
Richly laced with peace and fulfillment.

I do not expect
My future to be free of failure.
Nevertheless, Master,
I will try daily
To return this priceless life
Which you gave me
To your perfect rule.

This pledge I lift as grateful praise,
My Creator,
My Precious Savior,
My Eternal Guide.

Do not offer the parts of your body to sin, as instruments of wickedness, but rather offer yourselves to God, as those who have been brought from death to life; and offer the parts of your body to him as instruments of righteousness. Romans 6:13

PSALM 10

You have adorned the world, King of Glory,
In extravagant beauty.
With presumed judicial foresight,
Man has sub-divided land and sea,
Surrounding each region by boundaries.

In most resulting nations,
Decisions impacting residents
Are made by their local governors.

I am happy to be a citizen, Redeemer,
Of the country you chose for me.

True to the total pattern in your creation,
Its lovely scenery
Is immensely pleasing to the eye;
My liberty to choose,
Express preferences,
Chart my life course
Based on personal values,
Besides contributing opinions
On joint decisions for all of us,
Makes me thankful for where I live.

While enjoying these favors, Holy Father,
I have recognized a larger truth:
Whether for the span of a day or a life,
The place and situation
In which I find myself
Is always best for the satisfaction
Of my life's purpose.

I worship you, Divine Creator,
For your wise universal design.

"Are not two sparrows sold for a penny? Yet not one of them will fall to the ground apart from the will of your Father." Matthew 10:29

PSALM 11

When this adventure ends,
As it will, King of Kings,
You will walk with me
Through the entry
To the rest of eternity.

The essence of my earthly experience:
Lessons learned,
Knowledge gained,
Pleasures relished,
Sorrows mourned,
Challenges overcome,
Disappointments endured, and hopes fulfilled,
Will go with me,
None of it lost.

But, Master, the newborn joy to be tasted
At that homecoming
Will race through the epidermis
Of my changed body.
Then, I, too,
Shall shine brightly like the sun,

As radiant as a dazzling star,
Abiding with you forever.

"Blessed are those who wash their robes, that they may have the right to the tree of life and may go through the gates into the city."
Revelation 22:14

PSALM 12

God, my God, your love overwhelms me!
Of all sinful mortals,
Surely I am the worst.

While it's true I've never committed
The sin of murder,
Nor have I stolen
Cherished property
From another,
According to Jesus, I have participated
In a wrong that is equally evil.

While not technically removing
The spark of life,
Gossip diminishes
Joy in the life
Of its victim.

Though a charge of grand larceny
Might not be supportable,
The target of this sin
Is robbed of a good name
Which doubtless required
As much effort to build
As though it were material.

Yet goodness continues to rain down on me,
Your blessings too many to count.
Holy Friend, what justice system
Provides serial rewards for one
Who routinely treats divine decrees
As mere suggestions?

Compounding these specific transgressions,
I have corrupted the command
To love you,
With a counterfeit endeavor
To know about you,
Derived solely
From the thoughts and opinions
Of others.

This act leans blindly on the false belief
That learning the facts of biography
Produces relationship.

But it's been repeatedly proven
That commitment requires presence.
The content of the heart
Must be discovered at close quarters,
Frequently revealing shared passions,
Before a bond is forged.

At that point, love becomes a weaving,
Like strands of yarn in a tapestry;
You have taught us, Lord Jesus,
To aim for a goal of no gaps

Left in the pattern
By errant stitches.

Despite my blind failures,
You smile at me,
Overlooking my many mistakes,
Showering me with honors
As though I were flawless.

Thank you, God,
For your forgiving mercy.

 ..."Though your sins are like scarlet, they shall be
as white as snow."... Isaiah 1:18

PSALM 13

Lord, I love to rest in your embrace.
You are immovable, unchangeable;
My only true home is with you.

You promised to forgive
If only I ask.
I now humbly beg for your mercy, Father,
For my numerous acts of infidelity.

Inconsistent with my allegiance to you,
I have flirted with other gods.
In fact, I took many for test rides,
Only to discover
That none could make smooth
The inevitable bumps on life's road.

It was predictable that I would gravitate
To the altar of the god of fame.
Having always suffered a thirst for love,
I was easily pulled to this alleged deity,
Since he claimed ability to quench that need.
Some of the skills you have bestowed upon me
Seemed suited for presenting in his temple.
Worship came to a quick halt, Righteous Judge,
As you stripped the blinders from my eyes.

The mockery of my attempt to lead others
Toward humility, charity, and obedience,
As I prayed to receive personal prestige
For my efforts,
Abruptly became crystal clear.

This vision highlighted a tough lesson:
A desire for personal advancement
Cannot be masked
By a superficial appeal to others
That they honor you.
A mixture of confusion and guilt
Overwhelmed my hollow heart,
As stardom's effigy looked on,
Smiling knowingly.

Eternal Spirit, the world believes
Money fuels its engines;
The altar embellished with dollar signs
Is flamboyantly gilded.
Currency often appears
To make life easier, Jehovah,
Supporting mankind's illusion.
But I've never witnessed
Its permanent solution to life's problems.
It lacks the ability to counsel,
To inject the necessary thoughts
That inspire understanding.

You, however, have downloaded,
As audibly as a verbal prompt,
Healing concepts into my mind, Elohim.

In itself, the almighty dollar is lifeless.
But when buying sustenance for the needy,
Or underwriting the expense
Of valiant souls making you known
To the unknowing,
The very coins spent become sacred.

The god with the busiest altar
Has a three-way mirror at its center
Instead of a cross, Prince of Peace.
This idol is only glorified
When the worshiper's reputation
Is substantially magnified,
By fame, money,
Or even the misfortune of another.
This idea is irreconcilable
With your teaching,
Dependent as it is
Upon the faulty thinking
Of sinful man.

Guard me, El Shaddai, from fatal errors
In my acts of praise.
You are the one and only
Authentic God.

Teach me to worship you
Faithfully,
Endlessly,
In the same way in which
You love me.

"...If you are returning to the Lord with all your hearts, then rid yourselves of the foreign gods and commit yourselves to the Lord and serve him only, and he will deliver you..." 1 Samuel 7:3

PSALM 14

Holy Spirit

In my secret place, Eternal Lord,
You daily supply me
With a new measure of grace.
Into my lonely, hungry heart,
You stream an extravagant helping
Of your gentle, loving spirit.

Regardless of the current cause
Of my feeling of emptiness,
Your presence at my side
Heaps new hope
Into the gaping hole
At the center of my being.

With you, I encounter afresh
The staggering mystery
Of your consistent, inclusive,
Faithful forgiveness.
Grasping a concept as vast as your love
Would require several lifetimes
To completely embrace, Christ.

How can I fully process the idea
That your sacrifice centuries ago
Was payment in full

For every wrong thought,
Word, or deed
I will ever commit?

Is this the anomaly where
Seeming too good to be true
Does not prove that it is?

Messiah, my spirit is laden with sin.
At my very center lies totally exposed
An intractable selfishness,
A constant fixation on seeking first
What is best for me,
With little regard
For the interests of others.

Knowing so well my flawed nature,
You allowed yourself to be branded
With all of the evil I will ever commit.
More startling yet,
You accepted the punishment
Which should have been mine.

Ironically, I have always heard
A judge whispering in my ear,
Informing me of every one of my errors.

Righteous One, your system
Demands reflection on the stark contrast
Between mere morality and sacrificial love!

As towering bluffs on a yawning abyss
Leave a vast stretch
Of barrenness between,
Such is the chasm existing
Between good and evil.

On one ledge dwells a life
Absent of significant virtue, Son of God,
Though constantly aspiring
To achieve its highest attainment.

Across the divide is the perfect Spirit,
Lovingly surrendered
To advance the cause of others.

Thank you for your grace, God,
In continuing to love me,
Even as I linger
On the wrong ledge.

 For all have sinned and fall short of the glory of God, and are justified freely by his grace through the redemption that came by Christ Jesus. Romans 3:23-24

PSALM 15

Adonai, as I view a sunset,
Emblazoned in profuse shades
From your expansive pallet,
A metaphor for the human lifespan
Springs from the canvas into my mind.
Day is coming to an end.
Lying beside completed accomplishments
Appear fragmented tasks
To be resumed tomorrow,
Or forgotten.

A small portion of eternity has ended.

I recognize that
A twenty-four-hour slice of forever
Is a metaphor for my life.
Regardless of daybreak's revelation,
Calm sky or treacherous winds,
Dusk inevitably arrives, Dear Healer,
Followed by evening's darkness.
One more day is finished.

Eventually life, too, draws to a close.

Like King Hezekiah of old,
Indeed like most humans of today,
I long for an extension of my life.
Faith has removed the fear of death;
Yet I lack enthusiasm for dying.
Also, I shrink from being parted
From those whom I love.

For any day in question,
Whether brimming with excitement,
Racing by at break-neck speed,
Or dragging past in the doldrums,
Conclusion is unavoidable.

The same is true of a lifetime.

Indwelling Spirit, if we lull our minds
Into the expectation of a thousand years
As the balance in our time account
To enjoy, to struggle, to learn, to play,
A single segment of time loses value.
Conversely, if we obsess on life's brevity,
We will surely miss
The beauty of the present moment.

Would you have us approach each morning
WIth cheerful eagerness,
Totally free of dread or anxiety,
Greeting life with the certainty
That we will only encounter
That which you allow?

Oh God, let this view
Penetrate the core of my being,
So that life may become
Less tentative,
More lovely,
As I enjoy
A deeper communion with you.

"My days are swifter than a weaver's shuttle..."
Job 7:6

PSALM 16

Holy Spirit

Joy permeates my every cell, Gift of God,
When I am alone with you.
In solitude I hear your voice clearly,
Without having to sift
Through the cacophony
Of the world's chatter.
In this fragment of forever,
My spirit is refreshed,
My being renewed.

I could easily be persuaded
By the sweet thrill of our bond
To adopt monastic seclusion.

But you did not place me in a cloister,
Nor on a lonely island.
You obviously want me
Amidst the hustling,
Bustling masses of community.

All right then, King of Wisdom,
Send me out among your children.
Lead me to those
Whom you are drawing to yourself.
Grant me the privilege
Of holding their hands;

Soften my heart to respond lovingly.
Make me open to their needs.

Help me discover the best way
To lead my brothers and sisters
Into the understanding
That each one is your cherished child.
Teach me how to share the truth
That your individual plan for them
Far exceeds anything
Conceivable by man.

Guide me, Spirit of Truth, in prioritizing
The bits and pieces of each day,
So that my schedule
Always coincides with yours.

Allow me to serve your purpose -
Tilling the soil,
Sowing the seed,
Or nurturing the seedlings -
Whatever is needed
To bring you a bountiful harvest.

I praise you, Everlasting Father,
For loving me,
For calling me to assist
Your children in their quest for you.

 "...as for me and my household, we will serve the
Lord." Joshua 24:15

PSALM 17

I praise you, Reigning King,
For the perfect order
Of your plan for my life.

By this stage in my passage, however,
I had expected
More infirmity,
Less mobility,
More limitation,
Less mental acuity,
As an inescapable consequence
Of time.

Inwardly I behold no change
In that part of me
That truly is me.
Regrettably, Holy Friend,
The mirror's reflection
Is probably a more accurate picture
Of my genuine age.

I have dreaded many things in life;
Like others on that list,
Being older is not as difficult
As I expected.

Still, if you should ever consider
A minor modification to your plan,
I suggest a small sequential adjustment.
It might be worth considering
To allow humans
To enjoy at an earlier stage of life
The freedom and independence
Which accompanies retirement;
Maybe our minds and bodies
Would then be better suited
To respond to opportunities
As they occur during that time, Jehovah.

Gray hair is a crown of splendor; it is attained by
a righteous life. Proverbs 16:31

PSALM 18

Holy Spirit

Grace was a beautiful word, Lord of Hosts;
I had no idea what it meant.
I never doubted your sovereignty;
Unfortunately, however,
The image I had of you
Was of a divine judge
Draped in heavy, dark robes.

I viewed you as the eternal scorekeeper,
Recording my every mistake,
Willful or innocent,
Into an eternal ledger
With pages lacking a column
For extenuating circumstances.

I conceded death as inevitable.
However, I hoped that,
If you would someday deem me worthy, Adonai,
Heaven,
With its golden streets
Lined with choirs of angels
Awaits.

So my alpha task was to personally attain
Your standard of worthiness.

My only hope of pleasing you
Was in constant self-scrutiny,
Making any correction
Which would save you,
And me,
From eternal disappointment.

Sadly, the more I aimed at perfection,
The more convinced I became, Immanuel,
That simply calling myself a Christian
Did not make me innocent.

My failure was not
An error of behavior;
It was the blunder of not grasping
The incapacity of mortals for purity.
Despite that universal flaw,
Your eternal appraisal
Factors into the equation
The overriding principle
Of your unconditional and forgiving love.
Therefore, merely by virtue of my existence,
I am somehow accredited with profound worth.

Through my topsy-turvy view
Of your absolute rule over my life,
I had always expected judgment;
I had no illusion of mercy, Divine Ruler.

The day I met you for the second time
Was a day of all-out rejoicing!
The moment I knew you

For who you really are,
For one whose love is freely given,
I was truly born again!
Chronological age was instantly canceled,
Replaced by spiritual infancy;
Yet tucked into my swaddling clothes
Was the ageless assurance
Of your acceptance.

At that moment I knew with supreme relief
That you have always been
On my side, Lord Jesus!

I have disappointed you
More times than I can count.
Still, it is the "me" of me
Whom you cherish:
The little girl,
The wife,
The mother,
The grandmother,
The old woman,
In whom you see value!

Nothing prepared me, Teacher,
For the intense passion engulfing my heart
With this new understanding.

 ...who has saved us and called us to a holy life not because of anything we have done but because of his own purpose and grace. 2 Timothy 1:9

PSALM 19

More and more, Spirit of Christ,
My need for your company
Overshadows all else.

Your faithful protection is imperative
Whenever my radar detects a threat.
Whether the potential menace is life-changing
Or merely cause for inconvenience,
The very essence of me seeks
The haven at your side.

In other seasons, Son of Righteousness,
When my spirit rises to delight
By the good fortune of success,
My elation yearns for your companionship.

On really bad days,
When my best attempts don't measure up,
Feeling robbed of all hope,
My sole concentration
On dodging incoming darts,
I simply long for the reassurance
Of your arms.

Cuddling there,
I pour out my soul.

I praise you for the bounty
You continue to shower on me.
I confess the ways I daily fail you.
My thanks tumble out
For your forgiveness of my humanness,
With its self-centeredness
That produces tunnel vision,
As well as a propensity
For causing difficulty for others,
Shamefully unredeemed
By modest problem-solving skills.

Still, nestled in your gentle caress,
I feel our hearts beating
In an implausible oneness, Holy Father,
Given our lop-sided love.

 How great is the love the Father has lavished on us, that we should be called children of God! 1 John 3:1

PSALM 20

Holy Spirit

Righteous Judge, some of your children
Are difficult to hold dear!
To simply live alongside them
Is exhausting!

If I ever had patience
With him who complains incessantly,
I fear I've lost it, Lord of Lords.
Hearing him sigh, shriek,
Moan, and groan endlessly
Slackens the reins on my tongue.
It is re-shaped into a double-edged blade,
Shredding my restraint.
Doesn't he know
That others have problems, too?
Can't he see that some of his wounds
Are self-inflicted?
Has he ever considered seeking solutions,
Instead of voicing resentments?

Yahweh, must I love the braggart?
It's hard enough even to endure her.
Why must she constantly remind me
Of how beautiful and popular she is?
Everyone knows her children

Continually win prizes.
Their achievements are praiseworthy,
As is her husband's
Phenomenal business success.
But must she hammer me with the details?
Her hubris
Cripples my equanimity.

Is it possible to cherish
One who must micro-manage
All the people and circumstances
In his life?
Can he even imagine
The resentment he will harvest
From the presumption he has sown?
Has he thought of the talent he neglects
By ignoring the abilities of others?
Does he know that his commanding grip
Makes the rest of us feel strangled?

Counselor, I want to enjoy my sister,
The pessimist,
But doesn't she realize
The dreary veil she casts over others
By the dismal view of life
With which she clothes her spirit?
Can't she see the hopelessness
She inflicts upon any soul
Brave enough to share her space?
Real disaster elicits my quick compassion,

But why must she wince at agony
That has not yet arrived?

Every one of these is your child,
Just as I am, Abba.
The mission you assigned me
Is to love each one unconditionally,
As you do.

You have not appointed me
As their judge.
In the face of my irritation,
Please help me remember
Your call to continue to grow
Till I perfectly reflect
The character of your Son.

When the task appears more daunting
Than I even want to attempt,
Open my heart, Spirit of Grace,
To the certainty
That for someone,
I, too,
Am not easy to hold dear.

 Be kind and compassionate to one another, forgiving each other, just as in Christ God forgave you. Ephesians 4:32

PSALM 21

The sun, the moon,
The stars in the sky.
Clouds presaging
A weather change.
The tides working
In their unseen rhythm.

Storms so fierce
Many lives are lost.
Ensuing rainbows
Too gorgeous to savor, Lamb of God.

Bright sunny days
In peaceful meadows.
Brooks noisily trickling
Over sticks and stones.
Rivers churning
From the wellspring
To the sea.

Hustling, bustling man,
Self-important, Elohim,
In his pre-occupation.

You have invited us
As accompaniment on this journey
For our growing spiritual awareness.
Regrettably, few of us
Take full advantage
Of the invitation.

 "...Bring my sons from afar and my daughters from the ends of the earth – everyone who is called by my name, whom I created for my glory, whom I formed and made." Isaiah 43:6-7

PSALM 22

Father, I am weary.

My body feels a fatigue
Encompassing all its parts.
It transcends bone and tissue,
Penetrating to the core of me.

This exhaustion worms its way
Into my mind, Immanuel,
Taking my thoughts captive.
They have gone on strike
Like overworked and rebellious muscles.
Though awarded the singular honor
Of singing my life's song,
They refuse to even hum.

My psyche cries out for an intermission,
Insisting that without periodic rest,
The line I cast into the stream of life
Consistently comes back empty.

Regrettably ignoring this principle,
Some traitorous portion of my mind
Entertains an alien suspicion

That even brief inactivity
Permanently brands me as a sluggard.

Instead of fearing relaxation,
Teach me, Eternal Spirit, to embrace it.
Let me dive into the depths of tranquility,
Finding there a refreshing pond of inspiration
Where new creativity is born.

After you created all that is
From the chaos that was,
You sought respite.
Since I am made in your image, Lord of All,
Why does it surprise me
That I only function effectively
With regular intervals of leisure?

Everything you made employs this concept.
All the earth's greenery
Grows and blossoms in cycles;
A period of calm
Must occur between growth spurts.

Besides physical and emotional nourishment,
A newborn baby requires passing
Substantial portions of the day in slumber
To maximize development.
The notes in a magnificent musical score
Fail to produce the intended melody
Without planned rests
Contributing to the cadence.

On that first universal day of rest,
Gazing upon the extraordinary
Yield from your labor, Great High Priest,
Were you laying down the law
For continued creativity?
It's as if you were proclaiming
That recurring innovation
Does not spring from a drained spirit;
It is only generated
By refreshed insight.

With your sweet patience,
Teach me the rhythm
Designed specifically for my life.
Show me the balance
Between busy days and those of intermission,
As they combine to provide
My perfect tempo.

Divine Counselor, help me welcome
Each experience of stillness
As it renews my being,
Quickens my spirit, and strengthens me
For service in your kingdom.

"Six days do your work, but on the seventh day
do not work, so that your ox and your donkey
may rest and the slave born in your household,
and the alien as well, may be refreshed." Exodus 23:12

PSALM 23

My spirit languishes in the pit, Lord;
All hope is gone.

From my station in this long, dark tunnel,
My heart, burdened with sadness,
Struggling to combat trembling fear,
Beats out the cadence
Of a mournful dirge.

My soul begs for the misery to end.
Happiness seems forever gone.

I once communed with you, Spirit of Wisdom,
But the link has been strained
For some time,
Leaving me alone,
Lonely.

I wonder if people are laughing
Somewhere.
Are children playing
Somewhere?
Don't they know of my sadness?
Don't they care?

Messiah, my friend is dying.
Her long illness pointed to this day.
I've watched the earthly departures
Of others who have succumbed
To this antagonist.

At times like this, Jesus taught
I must ask for your help through prayer.
He said I should be persistent.
He described you as a loving Father
Who responds to his children's requests
Far more generously than any earthly parent
Could even attempt.

Jesus instructed that I should
Ask, seek, and knock.
I have prayed relentlessly
For Betty's healing.
I confess to being acutely confused.
You see, Rabbi, my heart still insists:
Surely one so pure,
So generous,
So loving as my friend
Must prevail
Against the brute that assails her.

My love for you
Declares I can rely on your mercy.

I have stored up numerous reminders
Of occasions when you have
Miraculously saved me

From desperate difficulty.
These memories engender assurance
That since your nature does not allow
Your response to your children to change,
You will once again come to the rescue,
Delivering your daughter
From the hungry jaws of Death.

Still, Spirit of Life,
You steadfastly refresh
My recollection
Of Jesus' full teaching
About answered prayer.
I hear him stress the enduring imperative
That all outcomes to our petitions
Must agree with your overall purpose.

I cannot pretend to know
What your final will for Betty is.
If, however, a healing of her illness
Is not part of your plan for her,
I feel certain,
Because she loves Jesus,
Of what the next stage of eternity
Will be for her.

I visualize her righteous spirit
Engrossed in her final battle --
The one we all will one day face.
Whatever else ensues,
I know that Christ,

The grand and holy Stallion
Who will carry each of us
To our eternal victory,
Will accompany her on the journey home.

Secured by your spiritual armor,
I perceive the certain destiny
Of faithful souls
Like my sister in Christ;
I have no concern
About her ultimate home.

At last, I watch my dear one
In her final moments on the planet.
Her eyes, Mighty Rock,
Are turned to the wall in surrender;
They reflect the gloating swagger
Of the vile,
Detestable demon of the universe
Towering over her.

His horrific image
Compels me to look away.
Then in a final show
Of loyalty to my friend,
I turn back one last time.

To my delighted amazement, Comforter,
The scene has shifted dramatically.
Her room is bathed in brilliant sunshine.
Incredibly, Betty
Has risen to her feet.

She ascends her magnificent mount;
The peerless stallion rises
On his powerful hind legs.
In a breathtaking instant,
His hooves leave the earth,
Soaring toward heaven.

Just before they disappear from sight,
My dear friend turns to look at me.
Her face is transformed.

Her eyes foretell the bliss
She knows she is about to experience,
Once in the presence
Of that angelic welcoming committee
From Paradise:
That great cloud of witnesses
Whom we have been promised.

Far beneath the heaven-bound pair,
Left shamefully behind
In a cloud of terrestrial dust
Sulks Death,
Proven impotent yet again,
Defeated for all eternity.

 ..."Death has been swallowed up in victory."
1 Corinthians 15:54

PSALM 24

Eternal Lord, what makes me think
I have properly kept the Sabbath
After sitting for an hour
On a comfortable pew,
Singing hymns, and hearing others
Share their understanding
Of who you are?

Did the few bills I dropped
Into the offering plate
Buy me a claim on obedience?

Moses instructed the children of Israel
To revere the Sabbath.
He commanded that it be kept holy.
You specifically decreed, he said,
That it be a day without labor.

In their commitment to the statute,
Your chosen people elaborated
On your Instructions, Adonai.
They studied your word,
Then expanded it extensively.
In great detail they specified

Activities which were deemed labor.
The result was a burdensome list of rules.

By stressing the idea
Of a work-free day,
They missed the larger concept
Of why you set this day apart
From the other six.

They ignored the special designation
You conferred on such a brief time span
By calling it holy.
Engaged in selfish thinking,
They failed to ponder
How they could dedicate the Sabbath
To express their gratitude
To you, Holy Creator.

However, after disparaging the failure
Of my spiritual ancestors
For adequately grasping
Your intentions for this day,
Tears of chagrin cleanse my cheeks.
I confess that I, too,
Have fallen short
Of devoting this day solely
To praising and thanking you.

My neglect does not pass without price.
I experience needless pain
By failing to connect the dots.

I'm left with an aching emptiness,
Traceable to failure
To provide the very least
That your steadfast love merits:
An endless expression of
Undying tribute and eternal acclamation.

Holy One, much like the grains of sand
From the vast barren spaces
The children of Abraham traversed,
The truth in your commands for Sabbath
Mysteriously slips through my fingers,
Robbing you of the praise
You should be receiving.

King Eternal, open my eyes
To the reason you made me:
To bring honor to you,
To glorify you with my highest tribute.

 "Remember the Sabbath day by keeping it holy."
Exodus 20:8

PSALM 25

Everlasting Father, I littered the path
To the foot of your throne
With numerous repetitions
Of the same thoughts,
The same deeds,
All clothed in identical hope:
This time would be different.
At long last I would find
The unity with you
For which I sorely yearned.

I'd somehow grown to view
My cherished perspective on truth,
Though unencumbered by fresh ideas,
As a medal earned for endurance.
I never suspected my closed mind
To be a nest for nurturing
The seeds of incorrigible weeds,
Effectively choking out
Any beautiful new thought
From the garden of my heart.

I guiltily admitted my countless sins,
While thinking them only normal
For imperfect mortals.

Still, I regretted each,
Praying for forgiveness,
Longing for pardon.
You graciously blessed my efforts,
Grossly out of proportion
To anything I deserved, Merciful Redeemer.

A major transformation came
When I realized I had been blind
To the necessity
In a life lived for you
To relinquish management authority.
I finally saw the need
To allow death by starvation
To my persistent hunger
To also direct the lives
Of the people I love.

I hadn't even dreamed
I must release all striving
In the name of self, Christ.
That only dawned on me
When I realized
That you are the prototype -
The pattern for me to follow.

My next discovery was seeing
The trait I most need to emulate
Is your humility.

I thirsted for spiritual growth,
But my study chiefly centered
On what scholars said about you.
How much more illuminating it is,
I now discern, King of Wisdom,
To directly download truth
Through your Son.

My spirit yearned for freedom
To soar like an eagle.
How delighted I was to learn
That is also your wish for me!

My best days are now spent
Watching you surgically remove,
Or at least seriously blunt,
The stingers from life's problems;
The amazing result
Becomes brand new solutions.

I consistently experience
Your living presence each day.
You hold my hand, Holy Friend,
Gently elevating my chin
With your forefinger;
Raising my awareness
By words inaudible to others;
Warmly hugging me close to your chest;
Correcting errant thoughts
With only a forgiving smile;

Mopping from my forehead
Drops of weariness and hurt;
Sweetly gazing
Into the deep recesses of my soul.

The union which I desperately desired
Has blessedly occurred,
Forged for all eternity.

"I am unworthy of all the kindness and faith-
fulness you have shown your servant."...
Genesis 32:10

PSALM 26

I am drowning in gloom, Lord of All.
Again I find a challenge
Boldly confronting me.

The product of yesterday's errors lives on.
Today is weighed down with anguish.
Tomorrow's dreams hide in the shadows;
Pain dwarfs all other sensations,
Arresting any potential pleasure.

Dwelling in my own personal valley,
My soul weeps in the darkness,
Totally void of resolution.
Dependence upon my own answers
Has only brought disappointment.

"Fear not; believe and follow me,"
Is your invitation, Jesus.
You have shown me that trusting you
Yields a happier life.
When I have given you all my cares,
I've witnessed the retreat
Of struggle and strain.
Hope returns,
Ushering peace into my heart.

So why, Spirit of Truth,
Don't I always rely on you?
Why do I habitually reclaim
Those trials, doubts, and sorrows
After having so trustingly
Laid them at your feet?

How often must I discover
That the excitement born
Of making my own decisions
Quickly pales,
As my soul is seduced
Down paths leading away from you?

Would not happiness be more assured
If your judgment ruled,
Rather than mine,
Leaving no room
For either choice or chagrin?
Yet I have finally realized
This would reverse your divine plan.
King of Glory, your heart yearns for me
To willingly trust you
In the face of adversity.

At last I understand
That my ultimate purpose
Is to shower you with praise and tribute.
Regardless of any other accomplishment,

If I fail in this,
It will be to my eternal shame.

Truth teaches that my forced obedience
Brings you no glory, Master.
Only voluntary surrender to your wishes
Displays my acknowledgement
Of your loving nature
For all to appreciate,
Bringing deserved acclamation to you.

I am grateful that
Even slow understanding is better
Than continued confusion.
I humbly ask you, Holy Spirit,
To continue to nudge me along,
Unveiling just what I need to know
For the next portion of the journey.
Then one day, I will arrive at your feet
With my heart in my hands,
Eagerly stretched out toward you.

 Whoever gives heed to instruction prospers, and blessed is he who trusts in the Lord. Proverbs 16:20

PSALM 27

The extravaganza that is your creation
On world-wide display, God Almighty,
Features every aspect
Of our marvelous planet.
Its splendor commands my awe.

Unfurled for universal admiration
Are manifold statements
Of your magnificent brilliance.

Viewing them inspires the arrival
In my throat
Of adjectives such as
"Exquisite", "magnificent",
"Dazzling", and "perfect".

It is like being transported
Into a front row orchestra seat,
Where I sit enraptured,
Hoping to win a backstage visit
With the playwright.

It would complete my life
To hear you share, Holy Creator,

The divine wisdom
That sired such beauty.

"...the living God, who made heaven and earth and
sea and everything in them." Acts 14:15

PSALM 28

At times my heart becomes entangled
In a twisted net of fear, Son of God.
The clinging, smothering nature
Of the restraint
Wrings from my throat
A reflexive cry of agony.

My volatile imagination spawns
Unruly thoughts;
My soul shudders
With dread and dismay.

I easily become amnesic, Yahweh,
Erasing from consciousness
My true identity as a daughter
Of the Master of the Universe.

Like the moving irony displayed
In the cruel image of a pitiful child
In an impoverished nation,
On whom physical starvation
Has inflicted an absurd resemblance
To an adult with a beer belly,
My poised appearance
Belies the inner fright
Hammering on the walls of my mind.

The cause of my torment, Holy Guide,
Is departure from trust.

As with a large number of your children,
At times I have grievously sacrificed
The calm of certainty
For the misery that accompanies
A fear of death.

Ultimately I grew to see
The incongruity in alarm
That my loving Father
Would blend anything hurtful
Into his plan for me.

That includes my transition
To the next phase of eternal life.

I now think of the adventure
As exchanging earth for heaven --
A gift, Immanuel,
Rather than a penalty.

I praise you for rescuing me from angst;
I thank you for your love,
Which provides assurance
For any time I slip back into despair.

 Trust in the Lord with all your heart and lean not
on your own understanding; in all your ways ac-
knowledge him, and he will make your paths
straight. Proverbs 3:5-6

PSALM 29

At this point on life's voyage,
The vigor of my once-young body
Has rebelliously departed, Christ.

Never the epitome of perfection,
I am now only a shell
Of my former self.

For anyone blessed
With great energy
Or pleasing presence, Paraclete,
Loss of these attributes
Must evoke great trauma.

I am grateful for your nearness
At times such as these,
When human frailty captures us,
Making us a prisoner
To our mortality.

I praise your reliable companionship,
Good Shepherd, as you hold our hands

While life takes a sudden detour
From the familiar path.

"I tell you the truth, when you were younger you dressed yourself and went where you wanted; but when you are old you will stretch out your hands, and someone else will dress you and lead you where you do not want to go." John 21:18

PSALM 30

Why am I here, Lord Jesus?
Is it my ego that insists
You have a specific purpose for me?

Of the myriad examples of your
Creative triumphs on the planet,
I must be among the least important.

Unlike the many facets of nature
Which the earth displays,
As well as persons
Who make a lasting influence
On the social order and other creatures,
My life is marked
By a lack of accomplishment.

My mind has lately
Been probing the possibility
That since your thoughts
Are not my thoughts,
Maybe a portrait of excellence
You might paint
Would be fundamentally different
From one that rolls off my brush.

Man's written history has featured
Dramatic discoveries and inventions;
Large numbers,
Especially regarding the size
Of that part of the race
An individual or group has affected,
Have constituted evidence of success.

However, Elohim,
What if your view
Of significant accomplishment
Is quite unlike man's?

What if your plan is less directed
Toward scorekeeping and stardom
Than we assume?
Could it be that our loving attitudes
Toward others, El Shaddai,
Present our most reverent worship?

Applying this different standard
To our analysis of achievement,
Was Abraham Lincoln's greatest deed
Saving the Union,
As marvelous an act as that was;
Or was his exceptional character
Best seen as he showed persistent caring
To a wife with mental illness,
Displayed by the respect and kindness
In which he dressed that love,
Even while busily conducting the war?

Did Winston Churchill please you more
By saving England from extinction,
Clearly a mighty and heroic deed,
Or by passionately warning his generation,
As well as all who followed,
Of the real existence and dangers of evil?

Was Mother Teresa's mission
More exceptionally met
By nurturing the sick and the poor,
Though she certainly filled
An enormous need by doing so,
Or by helping those same persons
Secure an avenue of communion
Directly to you through prayer?

You have taught me, Holy Friend,
That each soul counts mightily.
Are you, therefore, more impressed
By the authenticity of the love we express,
Or by the large number of persons we affect?

In reality, is the intentional,
Conscious concern of each one of us
For one another
The heart of your purpose for us?

 "For my thoughts are not your thoughts, neither are your ways my ways," declares the Lord. "As the heavens are higher than the earth, so are my ways higher than your ways and my thoughts than your thoughts." Isaiah 55:8- 9

PSALM 31

King of Wisdom, you are prime truth.
Your commands are not options.
Decreed by a spirit
Incapable of error,
They erase restriction and limitation,
By defining stability and certainty.

Before I knew your friendship,
You were the guardian of my forefathers.
You blessed Israel
By singling out souls
To be your messengers,
So the people of that nation
Could be the vessels
Through whom all of mankind
Would be favored.

Pledging devotion to you, Divine Ruler,
They built a homeland
Where they could freely express
Faith in you.

These pioneers bequeathed to me
An indwelling conviction
Of your unending kindness.

Your ceaseless companionship for all
Has been established and confirmed
Through successive generations.

You are my constant protector;
Your perpetual love
Is engraved in my core.
Through the darkness, Gift of God,
You stand sentry.
No permanent harm can reach me.

At every moment of the day
I feel your spirit,
As it reaches out to mine;
In every trial,
In every happiness
I feel your loving arms holding me.

 "I the Lord do not change. So you, O descendants
of Jacob, are not destroyed." Malachi 3:6

PSALM 32

Holy Spirit

It only takes a glance
At the stunning loveliness
Of your world
To see your majesty, Reigning King.
You truly are
The alpha and omega
Of all that is.

High mountains, deep oceans,
Magnificent forests, pristine lakes,
Each one a microcosm
Of your hallowed genius.

The variety of species
On land, in the air, and in the sea,
Spans the gamut of living beings
Arising from your brilliance, Holy Friend.

The most exciting jewel in your
Crown of creation
Is doubtless mankind.
Regardless of intellect,
Each individual person
Is a dazzling example
Of your divine design.

Thank you, Eternal Spirit,
For your extraordinary gift of being.

 God saw all that he had made, and it was very good. Genesis 1:31

PSALM 33

The boundless love for me
That flows from your heart, Abba,
Swells my being with wonder.

Devotion so encompassing
That it not only forgives,
But erases from memory
All images of guilt,
Can only dwell in the divine.

None but you, Lord of Lords, is capable
Of a compassion which looks past
My sin of this moment
To also absolve me
Of every future transgression
In thought, word, or act.

Your mercy cost dearly.
The price to you
Was the willing sacrifice
Of your only Son, Jesus.
His payment was the assumption
Of my guilt upon himself,
Including acceptance of my sentence:
Crucifixion.

Though by comparison my price
For receiving a clean slate
Was sharply discounted,
It inflicted a painful wound
To my pride.
It wasn't easy to confess the need
For a total cleansing of my soul.
Somehow, the attendant sip
From the cup of generalized humility
Failed to dilute my shame.

I was forced to admit the specific ways
I have failed you, Miracle Worker.

This exercise brought the realization
That I am not
Who I want to be.

Yet my surprise bonus
Was the astonishing revelation,
In light of all I had discovered,
Of your amazing delight
In who I really am.

This awareness evinced
The unvarnished truth:
I have no need to earn your approval.
It follows, therefore,
That it is no longer necessary
To compete for man's.

Consequently, unlike the multitude
Frantically struggling to be noticed,
I am now empowered, Divine Helper,
To honor the core of my being.

This lovely insight
Has brought a quiet peace
That wholly enwraps me.

 For it is by God you have been saved, through faith – and this not from yourselves, it is the gift of God – not by works, so that no one can boast. Ephesians 2:8, 9

PSALM 34

Lamb of God,
Supreme Omnipotence of the universe,
I pay tribute to you for salvation,
The zenith of your many wonders.

All of man's prizes on earth
Are given in reward for hard labor.
Your beautiful plan of resurrection
Seems counter-intuitive,
Out-of-step with natural law.

Sadly, Divine Rock, the command
For total surrender of our lives
To your control
Frequently delays,
For many of your children,
Even prevents for some,
Accessing incomparable peace,
The beautiful by-product of obedience.

But for any soul willing
To approach you with an open heart,
To intimately connect with you,
Belief that your righteousness is sufficient

To wash one clean in your eyes
Is the only requirement.

Miracle Worker, faith in the integrity
Of the one who invented truth
Demands little insight.
Your promise becomes a certainty
With only the daring to trust.

I praise and glorify you, Spirit of Christ,
For your "forever" prize,
Perpetual life in your presence.

 For the wages of sin is death, but the gift of
God is eternal life in Christ Jesus our Lord.
Romans 6:23

PSALM 35

God, you are huge.

Creator of all, large and small,
You are infinite,
Big beyond calculation.
I can neither weigh you
Nor wrap you in a measuring tape.
Like numbers without end,
You transcend
The boundaries of specifics.

While many things you have made
Are too small for the human eye to see
Without magnification,
Many others are recognized
For their enormity, King of Kings.

Steep mountain peaks
Reach high enough to touch the clouds;
Great oceans have a depth
Of many fathoms;
The sky is a stellar canopy,
Home of multitudinous astral bodies,
Stretching from one horizon to another;

Lush forests and jungles
Grow so thick
They are impenetrable;
Remote rivers
Snake along their courses,
Challenging navigation.
All are a reflection
Of your vastness.

Though your face remains unseen,
Your voice inaudible,
Still I am unshakably convinced
Of your existence, Adonai.
You are the Lord of the universe,
Committed to its precise operation.

Strange as it seems,
You also continuously display
A loving concern
For minute details of my life.
In crises where death threatens,
Or in matters of only trivial importance,
You show up.

Holy Friend, when opposing forces wound,
Causing deep pain;
When fortune smiles,
Propelling me
Into intense thanksgiving;
When you employ daily incidents
To correct my errant thoughts;

When the heavy blanket of sadness
Threatens to smother my spirit;
When energy and hope mix
A captivating cocktail;
When a barely perceptible churning
In the pit of my stomach
Abruptly develops into gripping fear,
You are here.

No matter the difficulty,
You apply a soothing balm, Divine Healer,
Like a mother's loving hand
Stroking my tormented brow,
Quelling misery's sting.

When I am seized by an artistic impulse,
Your guidance inspires me,
Providing passion and energy,
As I strain to exceed known limits
To fulfill your intent for me.

My joyful heart responds
To your companionship,
As you lift me
Beyond mere survival
To a place where
Brilliant sunshine is restored.

Your divinity blends the disparate scenes
That comprise my life
Into a single, meaningful whole,

Praising you
For my earthly adventure.

 "The eternal God is your refuge, and underneath are the everlasting arms. He will drive out your enemy before you, saying 'Destroy him!'"
Deuteronomy 33:27

PSALM 36

Holy Spirit

Divine Helper, when I need direction,
You are consistently trustworthy
To guide me toward wise decisions.
You are never bewildered,
Whether the question is complex
Or trivial.

Though omnipotent,
You graciously respect my views,
Frequently even allowing your wise rule
To be limited
By my unwillingness to accept it.

When my resistance results in an error,
You are a kind and loving shepherd,
Gently steering me back on course.
You have shown me that wandering
Can be greatly reduced
By narrowing my focus
To only you.

Grant me, Holy Father, the humility
To remember my immense need
For your loving parenting.
Endow me with the eager enthusiasm

To trade all that I think I know
For what you want me to know.

Instill in me, Immanuel, the awareness
That a life filled with peace
Is not the fruit
Of individual choices,
As much as it is the consequence
Of an unswervingly dedicated,
Securely abiding
Relationship with you.

"He who has compassion on them will guide
them and lead them besides springs of water."
Isaiah 49:10

PSALM 37

Eternal King, your blessings are infinite.
They cascade lavishly
In an abundant stream
For the pleasure of one
So undeserving as I.

For example, I am dazzled
By the efficiency
Of my body's performance
As it houses my spirit.

You designed a specific mind
Just for me.
Its functions are so intricate, so mysterious
That even now, after endeavoring for decades
I don't understand all it can do.
Each one of my organs has a particular job;
Yet its execution is performed
In agreement with all my other body parts.

Another exhibit of your creative kindness,
The resplendent globe,
Is the setting to some
For crime and violence,
Poverty and hunger.

Though these conditions are present,
I see them as challenges,
Not part of your intention, Elohim.

You dress this sphere
In essential splendor.
Fertile soil is plentiful
For man's tilling;
Partnership with
Rivers, lakes, brooks, and streams,
Abounding for irrigation,
Produces ample vegetation
For food and profit.
In gorgeous skies the sun reigns freely,
Beaming down rays of natural nourishment.
No matter the season,
Eden's greenery is always on view
Somewhere on the globe,
Affording perennial loveliness.

But the highest result
Of your divine imagination,
Oh, Messiah, is humanity.
Individual talents of your children
Astound me.
Like the unique print of one fingertip
Is the bit of genius living
In each person you formed.

When I survey the earth
With all its trimmings,

From inanimate landscape
To marvelous humanity,
I see it as your majestic gift,
For which I thank you, Eternal Lord.

 ...put their hope in God, who richly provides us with everything for our enjoyment. 1 Timothy 6:17

PSALM 38

In view of your unbounded power,
Your self-restraint
In controlling my life
Is remarkable, Jehovah.

You could have used puppetry
To insure my spiritual growth.
Life might have been simpler
Without choices.

However, like an insistent
But loving echo, Everlasting Father,
You remind me
That progress in the real labor
Of sanctification
Stems from making good selections.

I want my children to grow by my teaching;
I therefore enlighten them
Regarding the importance of wise decisions.
This will prove doubly beneficial
As they eventually realize the pleasure
With which their choices repay them.

I also want them to choose to love me,
Rather than doing so
Because of a script I have written.

Is that how you feel, Righteous Ruler?

I do love you.
I want all my ways to be directed
By you.

Though you do not require it,
As shown by your gift of freedom
In my selections,
I gladly yield them to you.

Please, Hallowed Teacher,
 So that all in my life
 Is in harmony with your design,
 Harness my reason,
 Which resolves vacillation;
 My tongue,
 Which gives voice to my thoughts;
 And my actions,
 Which issue from them.

In a world of ever-present danger,
 Where man's meager security
 Continues to prove deficient, Prince of Peace,
You alone offer the ultimate haven:
The permanent peace of eternity.

...I have set before you life and death, blessings
and curses. Now choose life, so that you and
your children may live. Deuteronomy 30:19

PSALM 39

Thank you for refusing
To give up on me, Gentle Savior.

My resistance to your plan
For eternal salvation
Nearly won for me
Perpetual destruction.

It seemed only reasonable
That living forever
With you in your home, Eternal Lord,
Required my highest effort.

Fortunately, and after much striving,
A realistic analysis
Of my habitually poor behavior
Coaxed and cajoled
My nervous work ethic,
Softened and soothed
My longing but frustrated heart,
Finally bringing peace;
The bonus was my reverent acceptance
Of the fruit of your grace.

The mission is accomplished, King of Glory;
My future is secure.
My eternal praise to you,
For seeing virtue in me
I never knew existed.

What wonder!
What serendipity!
What an epiphany!

 "...you are a gracious and compassionate God, slow to anger and abounding in love, a God who relents from sending calamity." Jonah 4:2

PSALM 40

Holy Spirit

Living on this planet, Son of Man,
With several billion scarred souls
Like me,
I continue to discover
What irreparably broken beings
We are.

Too long blinded to reality,
I labored with the torment
That to join you in heaven,
I must register a spotless score
In earth's schoolroom.

Lord of All, my early memories highlight
A precept centering on a single rule:
My physical efforts must produce
A soul morally fit
For residence with you.

To live with you,
I must almost
Be you.

This erroneous idea
Produced a ready willingness

To listen to the incessant seduction
Of earth's diabolical prince.
He constantly insisted that with
More effort,
More prayer,
More study,
I could arrive at that perfect state
Which mirrors yours.

One stunning morning,
A brilliant dawn awoke my consciousness
To the awareness that,
Though I truly am indelibly stained,
From the depth of each dismal failure
To the tip of my brightest endeavor,
None of that matters to you.

Neither my sinful condition
Nor my presumptuous idea
That I could become perfect
Through human effort,
Frustrates your
Unearned,
Stubborn
Love for me, Son of Righteousness.

Beyond belief then,
Still unimaginable now,
In spite of my brokenness,
You love and accept me.

Admission into your kingdom
Is a free gift.

You loved me before my birth;
Nothing I can ever do,
Will shake your devotion.

In return, you only ask, King of Kings,
For my love,
Expressed by my total dependence upon you.

The pathway into your kingdom
Is finally revealed when I admit the truth:
My heart is corrupt,
Because perfection is beyond human reach.

That essential step,
Requesting your help,
Is the easy part.
With joy I see, Eternal Judge,
Your assistance has already arrived
Through your Son's redemptive sacrifice.

My best move is to praise and thank you,
Since your response
Is a completed deed, Indwelling Spirit.

 Jesus said to the woman, "Your faith has saved
you; go in peace." Luke 7:50

PSALM 41

As part of your original creation,
Holy Creator, you fashioned heaven
As my ultimate destination.
Even now you are preparing
A place for me there.

All through my life
You have afforded me
Ceaseless, caring provision.
So I try to picture the sanctuary
To which I shall transition
Through the gift of death.

On our planet, the beauty you created
Is unrivaled, Messiah,
By anything man has ever built.
Lovely as it is,
It offers only a shadow
Of what awaits me in your home.

If I were an artist,
A breathtaking canvas,
Replete in infinite shades
Of vibrant hues,

Would display my expectations
Of that marvelous everlasting home.

If I were a musician,
A symphony composed in a major key,
Featuring a wide array
Of stringed instruments,
Would offer only a hint
Of the harmony I will forever enjoy.

Sadly, I lack those artistic gifts.
To project a vision
Of our everlasting home, Spirit of Wisdom,
I must construct a mosaic
By merging the verbal image
Revealed in your Holy Word,
With the sketch inferred
By your personal qualities,
Which have become real to me
Through our growing friendship.

Christ, I believe the fruit of my effort
Truly reflects
The magnificence I shall enter
A nanosecond after laying aside
This feeble wreckage
Which has cradled my spirit
During its visit to earth.

As amazing as this planet is,
Surely your home

Will be beyond wonder.
Once there, I am certain
I will be reunited with dear ones
Momentarily lost in a variance
Of individual itineraries.

When I next see them, Eternal Spirit,
Perhaps your divine sweetness
Will provide an opportunity
During our homecoming for
Forgiveness,
Where wounds remain;
Words of gratitude,
Where previously unspoken;
A full expression of love,
Where formerly constrained;
Spontaneous, untethered release,
To a soul thirsting for freedom;
As well as any other missing statements
Which have prevented closure.

Holy Friend, regardless of the scenery,
No matter who else is present,
I have one guarantee:
There I shall live
Forever with you.

Through my friendship with Jesus,
I have sometimes felt you near, Abba.
Each of these events has been
An intensely meaningful encounter,

But a ruefully rare occurrence.
They always made me long for more.

In that land of tomorrow, Holy Guide,
I believe the occasional inspiring incident
Will become the continuing certainty.

Though I search for details,
I suspect the heart of eternity
Is in the query:
Is heaven a place,
Or is it a presence?

 He will wipe every tear from their eyes. There will be no more death or mourning or crying or pain, for the old order of things has passed away. Revelation 21:4

PSALM 42

Lord of Lords, the curtain rising
On the drama of my life
Reveals a cast costumed in love.
The playwright plies dialogue and action
To showcase tranquility and hope;
The story line sets forth
A tale abounding in blessings.

As leading lady, it is now incumbent upon me,
Though hugely humiliating,
To finally confess my lack of gratitude
For your habitual generosity.
In fact, your enduring kindness
Has paradoxically raised the bar
On my audacity,
Seemingly directing me to
Relentlessly require only bright outcomes
In my life.

In sharp contrast, Light of the World,
When I do encounter a modest obstacle,
Cranial alarm bells scream.
At each minor frustration,
Dour consequences are expected.
Even a brief visit in a valley of shadows

Evokes ascendant anguish.
In truly serious trouble,
Alien and malignant visions
Completely hijack my senses.

Strangely, as I try to discern
Cause and effect,
From the depths of my mental morass
Arise thoughts draped in irony,
Giving birth to unfamiliar questions:

Why am I so slow, Divine Teacher,
To praise and thank you
In my happiness,
Yet promptly present you
With the bill for all my pain?

Has my soul become blind to the fact
That failure to declare appreciation
In the good times
Is the unwitting parent
Of at least some of the bad times?

I clearly need your Son's sacrifice
To cleanse this explicit sin.
My presumptuous attitude,
Which ignores my many flaws,
Leaves my only hope for eternal life
In your view of my heart,
The basis of your salvation plan.

Nevertheless, Lord of Peace,
With this calming certainty,
There is no room for doubt
That your promises are true.

Therefore, I've learned
It is safe for me to surrender
My insistent demand to know
The answers to all questions,
The solutions to all puzzles.
It is my act of love
To suspend contemplation,
Releasing everything
To the sweet,
Healing
Assurance
Of
Trust.

...Sing and make music in your heart to the Lord, always giving thanks to God the Father for everything, in the name of our Lord Jesus Christ. Ephesians 5:19-20

PSALM 43

What an extraordinary blessing, Jesus,
Is your forgetfulness.
It is the automatic bonus
That keeps on giving
Each time you forgive my sins.
Exclusively divine,
This trait is sadly absent
In your children.

Master, whenever I harm someone,
My soul grows parched and dry
With thirst for the absolution
That also forgets the sin.
As the perpetrator, in its absence
I am more deeply grieved than
If I had been the victim.

The injured party's brooding focus
On my transgression
Exhibits true unwillingness
To forgive.

But my aptitude for freeing another
Is no more readily accessible, Abba.
When offended,

I too often aim to wring out
The last drop of regret
From the guilty person.

Your profound mercy, however,
Is instantaneous.
Because of Christ's sacrificial act,
Before I utter
The last syllable of confession,
I am completely redeemed.
The incident is deleted
From your remembrance.

Merciful Father, my gratitude
For declaring me innocent,
In the face of significant evidence
To the contrary
Is beyond my faculty for expression.

But even more exceptional
Is your graciously replacing
The memory of my wrong doing
With my portrait as the embodiment
Of pure innocence, Blessed Redeemer.

..."For I will forgive their wickedness and will re-
member their sins no more." Jeremiah 31:34

PSALM 44

Lord of Hosts, your gracious heart
Holds a vision of me
Far more exciting
Than my wildest dreams could portray.

Through the biological process you created,
Each individual is called into existence
With uncommon blessings.
Rightly consecrated for use,
They provide a wondrous opportunity,
Following the leadership
Of the Indwelling Spirit within,
To achieve outcomes which bless all.
This is realized through
Sound personal selections made
Over a lifetime.

However, Blessed Redeemer,
This single facet of your plan
Is often the trapdoor through which
Many of us so easily
Fall into failure along the way.

My obstinate pride
In an inherent right to choose
Fails to even hint at how difficult
It is to make good choices.

How it must sadden you, Father God,
When my decisions are unwise.
How tiresome to your ears
Must be the hubris I display
By complaining of the consequences
To which my own desires introduce me.

Poor judgment escalates to sin
When I reject responsibility
For the unhappy fallout.

As a result, my character is reshaped,
Becoming considerably less attractive.

On those rare occasions, Holy Spirit,
When I take my thoughts captive,
Carefully considering all available options,
I am amazed at the lovely harvest reaped.

Lord Jesus, when you walked on this planet,
Your tender teaching focused
On the disappointing failure
When trying to alter conduct
Without first transforming the heart,
From which all actions flow.
You showed me that my deeds
Are the children of my attitudes.

Lasting behavior modification
Requires spiritual heart surgery.
Help me stop whining over difficulties;
Instead, Lamb of God, let me embrace
The power you offer
To take charge of circumstances
By becoming accountable for
My role in their origin.

Teach me to choose well
When possibilities are many;
Or when the apparent best
Seems illogical;
Or when the rightness of a selection
Is eclipsed by the gut-wrenching pain
Which accompanies it.

Remind me that my best decision
Is always the one that demonstrates
My love for you.

Tweak my remembrance of your forever love.
Assure me that depending on you
As my eternal Lord
Is not only the right choice,
But the smart choice.

Submitting to you, King of Kings,
Allows me to lean
On your superior strength,
Rather than my puny power.

You, my brothers, were called to be free. But do not use your freedom to indulge the sinful nature; rather, serve one another in love. Galatians 5:13

PSALM 45

Though this trial rigidly persists
Against the strength
Of ordinary answers;
Though the quagmire
Through which it drags me
Exhausts my spirit,
Boggles my mind,
Wrings the last tear
From my heart;

Nevertheless, Lord,
I praise you.

Though others on whom I depend
Seem unimpressed,
Uninterested,
Even unfeeling;
Though evil forces ridicule me;
Though shamefully betrayed
By a runaway mind
Which rebelliously deems
The Enemy's reasoning credible;

Nevertheless, Great High Priest,
I trust you.

You walked this earth
Clothed in a body like mine.
You tasted the zenith
Of physical pain.
You endured absolute desertion,
Not only by friends,
But by God himself;

Nevertheless, Christ,
You braved the misery.

When I scream, "I hate this!"
You recall your utmost test.
When my spirit is overcome by fear,
You re-live your anxiety
At Gethsemane,
Where you sweated drops of blood.
When I brood on injustice,
You remind me
Of the Father's outrage
At man's sin.
You have lived my suffering
And so much more;

Nevertheless, Holy Friend,
You fulfilled your mission.

Though each day brings
Unending questions
I cannot answer,
I rest in the peace

Of understanding
It isn't necessary
That I understand.
Though calendar pages turn quickly,
Leaving a shrinking instant
For action;
Though there remains
A multitude of tasks
To which I feel called;

Nevertheless, Eternal Father,
Into your hands I commit my spirit.

It is good to wait quietly for the salvation of the Lord. Lamentations 3:26

PSALM 46

Holy Spirit

Weak mortals that we are,
When we believe we have attained
The status of developed souls,
We can then be certain
We are merely wandering waifs, Elohim.

During the early years of love
Between my soul mate and me,
We foolishly presumed ourselves
Spiritually grown-up.
Lacking almost everything necessary
For authentic maturity,
Selfless love still
A stranger to our hearts,
We were doubtless little more
Than children grown tall.

In addition, we readily confess
To committing all of the mistakes
Most young parents fall prey to.

This admission contributes, Holy Friend,
To our delighted shock
When viewing our descendants today.

We are blessed by this collection
Of breathtaking beings,
Displaying a wealth of intelligence,
Charming spirits, and giant hearts,
Plus an abundance of physical grace,
As they add to our past
Their layer of exceptionalism.

There can be only one explanation
For these embodied superlatives:
Your godly magic!
Thank you, Righteous Magician.

Know therefore that the Lord your God is God; he
is the faithful God, keeping his covenant of love
to a thousand generations of those who love him
and keep his commands. Deuteronomy 7:9

PSALM 47

Are you broken-hearted, Holy One,
When I fail to live in accord
With the people in my life?
Do you grow weary
Of my inability to recognize
That you placed them here?

If I could truly fathom
Your unwavering endurance
In loving me, King Eternal,
Would I finally,
Once and for all,
Release the need
To compete
With anyone for anything,
Especially your love?

As I bask in the wonder of your grace,
Would I also be able to accept
That I am not your only child?
That the extravagant love
You pour on me
Is given equally
To all who believe in your Son?

Would this new insight
Soften my heart sufficiently
To confer legitimacy
On opinions that conflict with mine?
Could I even celebrate the success
Of one who dislikes me?

Does the greatest source
Of my suffering
Stem from abiding
By the world's values,
Instead of yours, Rabbi?

Does my enslavement
To material possessions
Induce me to cling fiercely
To what should be held gently?

Does my greed
Deny me the joy found
In blessing those with less
Out of my abundance?

Do you mourn when I wrap the famous
In a mantle of importance,
Thereby forfeiting the thrill
Of discovering splendor
Hidden in the humble?

Are you pleased, Lord of All,
By my use of time?
Have I become so allured by technology
That I only see the sparkle,
Overlooking its addictive property,
Fraught even with the power
To dilute my commitment to you?

When I inventory my human failures,
My heart is engulfed with gratitude
For the merciful forgiveness
You grant one as weak as I.

"You did not choose me, but I chose you and ap-
pointed you to go and bear fruit – fruit that will
last." John 15:16

PSALM 48

Does it pain you, Holy Teacher,
Or do you find it merely amusing
To see my frantic search for you,
When you are not lost?

Nor has eternal truth vanished.
At times, however, I unfortunately allow
The delicate strands of life's lessons
Which you have previously taught me
To slip, unnoticed, from my grasp.

You gave me a physical body
Where your sacred spirit
Was designed to dwell.
If only I had cared for this treasure
As you directed.
Grievously, my sin-stained thinking
Has led me to serious misconceptions
Regarding your gift
And my responsibility to it.

Since the substance of my physical form
Is primarily living flesh,
You instructed me concerning
The stewardship of this holy vessel.

Your revelation has set sensible rules
For its maintenance.

Does my ignoring your training
Challenge your love and mercy?
Is the body's functional breakdown
The inevitable result?

When I focus on external beauty
In myself or others,
Overlooking loveliness of spirit,
Do you want to shake some sense into me?

Do I cause you sorrow, Lord of Peace,
By thinking my body
Is the total sum of who I am?

This irreverent idea
Not only raises my anxiety
At every hiccup in its performance;
It unmasks a casual amnesia
Of your long-range plans!

You sent your Son Jesus
To deliver to me and the whole world
An invitation to eternity.
You would not have made
Such a sweeping offer
Had you been incapable
Of assuring its fruition.

Though it brings me sadness,
I must often reluctantly acknowledge
The weakness of my faith.
This failure emphasizes
My urgent need to transform
My expectations of your dependability.

Were I to fully wrap my mind
Around the truth as you declare it,
Would I more readily recognize
Your sheltering hedge of protection
Surrounding me,
Guarding from any lasting danger?

Regardless of my best efforts,
The dregs of uncertainty
Do, at times,
Creep into the hidden corners
Of my heart.

For the future, Holy Guide,
I pledge on these occasions
To depend solely
Upon your eternal righteousness.

As long as you live,
So shall I.

Fight the good fight of the faith. Take hold of the eternal life to which you were called when you made your good confession... 1 Timothy 6:12

PSALM 49

Holy Friend, it is so easy,
So natural,
To trust you,
Now that I know you.
Understanding your nature
Strengthens the blessing of our union.

Under bright skies or bleak,
No matter how often I fall down,
No matter whom I disappoint,
Though I frequently fail to grasp
What you want me to know,
You are my Lord.

You are prime wisdom:
You've taught me incredible truths.
You are unrivaled strength:
You've inspired me
To face relentless enemies.
You are love without condition:
During every conflict,
I feel your attentive care, Comforter,
You are shelter in the fiercest storm:
I've turned to you
When there seemed no safe haven.
You are light in the darkest tunnel:

A radiant sunrise
Has always peeled back the gloom.
You are unfailing companionship:
Like the closest of friends,
You encourage my best effort.
You are always available, Almighty God:
Do you even have voice mail?
You are a constantly listening ear
Who never interrupts:
You even hear thoughts yet to be spoken.
You are a shield from all fears:
My heart still marvels
At your most recent rescue.
You are a fervent cheerleader, Savior:
You yearn for my success.
You fill all my needs:
I've never lacked anything truly necessary.
You are a brilliant, stimulating teacher:
You gently lead me through
The ache that often precedes learning.
You are the gatekeeper of my experiences:
You grant entrance
To only those circumstances,
Both delightful and difficult,
Best suited to prepare me
For dwelling with you eternally, Great Rock,
Ground of my hope.

Every good and perfect gift is from above, coming down from the Father of the heavenly lights, who does not change like shifting shadows. James 1:17

PSALM 50

Holy Spirit

Someday my exciting sojourn
Amidst the multitudes
Upon this terrestrial orb
Will conclude.
Instantly, my spirit
Will be directed forward,
To the next encounter
Along this cosmic passage.

As always, Everlasting Father,
The prime component of that event
Will be your presence at my side,
Bearing, as you unfailingly always have,
The burdens that are just too heavy
For me to suffer.

The transition
From the life I have known
Into the upcoming segment
Of limitless time
May be difficult.
Few share Enoch's experience,
Bypassing death's pathway to heaven.

Yet, like climbers trudging the steep path
To the mountain's peak,
Once I arrive home, I know I shall find it
Well worth any struggle required.
How magnificent it will be
To reside in a place without barriers,
In a body free of affliction.

Exciting beyond words
Will be the reunion
With those I've known and loved,
With those I've loved but never known,
In your presence for all time, Lord Jesus.

 Now we know that if the earthly tent we live in is destroyed, we have a building from God, an eternal house in heaven, not built by human hands. 2 Corinthians 5:1

PSALM 51

Spirit of Life, I am barely alive,
In a gloomy, shadowy basement of despair.
The tainted air blown in
By the winds of dread and loneliness
Takes the path through my nostrils
Straight to my lungs.
Sadly, it passes no site en route
Where endorphins might be released,
For a possible lift of my spirits.

The bright sunshine of yesterday
Has vanished,
Taking hope
As its traveling companion.

The enemy without,
Allied by his lieutenant within,
The ugly monster strategically situated
To feed on the smallest crack
In my self-confidence,
Mounts a two-pronged offensive
On my mind, Adonai.

His troops batter my reason,
Driving me into abject fear.
Physical and emotional pain

Take my thoughts captive.
I have but a faint memory of peace.

Occasionally, like a crocus
Sprouting in springtime,
My forgotten optimism
Peeks through earth's clods of doubt,
But intense anguish promptly
Tamps it down again
Beneath the sticky soil of cynicism.

An elusive reminiscence of past happiness,
Downgraded almost to nostalgia,
Is shoved aside
By this malevolent inner beast
So that even the tiniest bud of recall
Is forced to retreat.

Only by straining every fiber
Of tenacity I retain
Can I vaguely rekindle
Thoughts of brighter days.

That was when my body,
Graced by vibrant health and energy,
Joyfully housed a spirit
Filled with faith;
When my mind was the home office
For unending creativity;
When my sole purpose in life

Was to know you, Holy Healer,
To become your friend.

Thankfully, even amidst the gloom
Of pain and misery,
Your Holy Spirit gently reminds me:

There is still one who cares:
One larger than life;
One greater than grief;
One who overcomes doubt;
One whose judgment is softened by mercy;
One who graciously whispers acceptance
Into the nooks and crannies
Of the human heart;
One who protects all who love him
With a host of defending angels;
One who fills all needs
Without being asked;
One directing each life with care
To the smallest detail
As closely as he governs
The faultless operation of the universe;
One who lived
Before the human mind can remember,
Who will exist after all minds cease.

Even in this anguish, Almighty Rock,
My hurting heart
Looks hopefully to you
With breathless wonder.

"For the Lord your God is the one who goes with you to fight for you against your enemies to give you victory." Deuteronomy 20:4

PSALM 52

Wonderful Counselor, help me to see
How persons born and raised
"On the wrong side of the tracks",
Living one bread-and-margarine-supper
Away from starvation,
Manage to nurture children
Rich in faith, vision, and grit.

History has demonstrated this anomaly
Again and again.
Millions who were given
Only a meager shot at life
Have hit the bull's-eye of success.

My family and those of friends,
Despite residence
On the outskirts of respectability,
Hammered out the mold
For good and faithful people
To replicate,
No matter the obstacle.

This, Good Shepherd,
Is one of your miracles.
In addition to the toil and resolve

Demonstrated by the dedicated,
You have empowered each of us
By impartially implanting in our hearts
The seed of success.

Jehovah, thank you for your blind love
That sees excellence in everyone.

"... God does not show favoritism but accepts men from every nation who fear him and do what is right." Acts 10:34-35

PSALM 53

Holy Friend, I celebrate
Your guidance through the decades.

Starting before I really knew you,
Despite my stubbornness
You have taught me
To welcome your wisdom
Into my heart.

I worship you, Immanuel,
For tearing down
My wall of self-will.
If only unquestioning acceptance
Had been my default setting,
Much time would have been saved,
Many unpleasant detours avoided.

Any spiritual growth
That has been achieved
Is only due, Holy Teacher,
To your enduring instruction.

I continue to bask
In the bright glow
Emitting from supreme reason,

As you patiently stream it
Into my mortal mind.

Yahweh, it is my thrill
To shout a joyful doxology
To your love!

 Glory in his holy name; let the hearts of those
who seek the Lord rejoice. 1 Chronicles 16:10

PSALM 54

Holy Spirit

Life is a love song, Lord of Lords.

Its original music and lyrics
Were composed by you,
As a dedication to the potential
Of beautiful possibilities
For each soul you create.

At the instant of conception,
A triumphant fanfare sounds,
Leading into the overture
Of a glorious symphony.
Its theme is celebration,
For another new vessel
Has been born, Divine Virtuoso,
Through which you wish
To express your love.

However, even when the new heart
Is wrapped in the delicate harmony
Of your masterful opus,
At its center, Christ,
It is sadly marred
By a hidden cavity
Of emptiness.

Your sacred plan requires
An interconnection
Between all of your creatures;
You therefore wrote a score
Composed of heavenly chords
To evoke a spontaneous flow
Of mutual love.

But the inherent hollow
Found in the heart
Of all newly born mortals, Son of God,
Has grown in strength,
Rewriting your magnificent melody
Into a discordant,
Jarring noise
That permeates the land.

Besides lacking its pre-ordained beauty,
The resulting sound proves ineffective
In making an even more vital bridge
For each of us:
A link to you, God Almighty,
Essential to empower and sustain
Your children
During their visit to earth.

An ensuing mysterious lament
Now abounds *sotto voce*,
Its plaintive melody
Grieving the void
Where expectation would suggest,

Adonai, at least an idea
Of what it is that is missing.

In spite of the song's distraction
Caused by the sad but universal deformity,
At the genesis of each life
A compelling bond sprouts,
Buds,
Comes to full flower,
Uniting the soul you chose
To share in the wonder of creation
With the life growing in her body.

A lilting lullaby,
Like a soft caress,
Drifts between the two,
Mother and infant,
An extemporaneous duet of devotion
To new life and new love.

With the passage of time,
Fresh affinities are orchestrated
For the child, El Shaddai.
New alliances emerge,
Some platonic, others passionate,
Many passing, perhaps a few perennial,
Encouraging participation
In the world's social order,
Always based on personal relationships.

Recognition of commonality,
A penchant shared with another,
Creates a harmony
Conveying consonance.
Even such a purely human tie
Lifts the spirits
Of this twenty-first century model
Of your eternal design.

But still, Eternal Spirit,
The heart's empty cleft remains,
Emphasizing its basic pathology:
Obsession with self.

Life's whimsy
With its erratic tension --
Today's *crescendo*,
Tomorrow's rest --
Sparks the sense
Of a missing note
In the composition's meter.

A strangely mournful refrain,
Like a rhapsody in quest
Of undefined fulfillment,
Hums in the breeze, Eternal Lord.

Eventually,
As your spirit beckons
With a magnetism
That is only ignored

At great peril,
Your precious creature
Scores a sorrowful ballad,
Finally confessing the need
For a nexus to the Prince of Peace.

A love song dedicated to you,
An answer to your call
At life's beginning,
Is gloriously modulated
Into an exultant alleluia --
Triumphant praise
To the one
Who alone replenishes,
Redeems,
Satisfies authentic needs,
Making your creature,
At long last,
Whole.

Rabbi, I marvel at the process
By which you heal a defective soul,
Transforming it to completeness.
I wonder at the patience
Which flows from your heart,
Continuing to bless with joy,
Transposing a dissonance of sound
Into a symphonic movement,
Swelling in jubilant excitement

From one movement to the next
Until the finale.

I pray that a modicum of that same quality,
Patience,
Be instilled in your creature.
Let that dear one
Dig in for one more measure, Holy Friend,
Holding on to the strain,
Clinging to whatever degree of faith
Has been thus far received.

The glory of the reprise
Will be well worth the wait,
As you divinely mend the heart
With your love song.

This is love: not that we loved God, but that he
loved us and sent his son as an atoning sacrifice
for our sins. 1 John 4:10

ARE YOU LOOKING FOR A FRIEND – A VERY SPECIAL FRIEND?

One who is always there for you? Who's never too busy?

One who, if you lose your way, lovingly shows you a better path?

One who appreciates humor and recognizes how its presence in life enhances your joy?

How about a friend who is constantly accessible? E-mail and cell phones connect us to human friends when they're available. But they often cannot be reached. That's never true of the Father, the Son, and the Holy Spirit.

Reading "My Holy Friend", you will learn the truth that has changed millions of lives – that the majestic, sovereign God of the Universe wants to be your Best Friend.

JOY RASH has devoted a major portion of her life to writing and presenting Christian programs and Bible studies. Her ministry has included the publication of stories and Sunday School lessons for children. As a current resident of Arizona with her husband, Joy continues her efforts to respond to Christ's Great Commission (Matthew 28:18-20) by providing weekly Bible studies on her website, **JoyInChrist.weebly.com**

She considers one of God's greatest blessings the gift of her three sons, three daughters-in-law, thirteen grandchildren, and two great-granddaughters.

CPSIA information can be obtained
at www.ICGtesting.com
Printed in the USA
FSOW04n1441060715
8568FS

9 781478 735007